Investing

This Book Provides A Comprehensive Understanding Of Investments, Offering Valuable Insights And Advice For Both Novice And Experienced Investors To Enhance Their Financial Future

Titus Dennis

TABLE OF CONTENT

Choices Terms For Seller And Buyer

Certain words refer to options traders. We might refer to the traders as buyers and sellers in other contexts. Nevertheless, a more technical phrase is employed in the context of options trading.

Writer: An investor who owns and is selling an options contract is referred to as a writer. The buyer will pay the writer a premium when they sell the option. The right to purchase a certain number of shares at a striking price will be purchased by the buyer.

Holder: Essentially, a holder is an investor looking to buy an options contract. Upon purchasing an options contract, a call options holder will get the right, subject to certain conditions, to buy the underlying stock. All rights to sell the underlying stock belong to a put holder.

In an options transaction, a writer and a holder are often on different sides of the trade. While the other signs up, one writes an option. But the kind of losses to which these two are vulnerable distinguish them most from one another.

Members enlist to acquire the option, but not the duty, to buy or sell shares. They are given the freedom to decide when and if to exercise their right under the terms of the contract they sign. They are free to renounce the agreement and let it expire if the option eventually goes out of the money. They will only lose the setup fee for the options contract in such a case.

However, things are different. Writers, for example, need to be more flexible. The writer must accept the order and execute it by selling the shares at the current strike price if a call option holder chooses to exercise their right. In the event that the writer does not own all of the shares in a contract, they will need to be bought at market value and sold to the holder at the strike price. The writer is required to bear any losses that may occur.

Since writing entails significant risk, it is advised that novices limit their investment to stock options once they have accumulated enough experience over time.

How Do ETFs with Dividends Operate?

A dividend-paying exchange-traded fund makes investments in a number of dividend-paying equities. The fund will aggregate the dividend payments from various stocks into a sizable dividend fund, which it will, after that, distribute to exchange-traded fund investors in accordance with the number of shares each investor owns. Remember that not every exchange-traded fund will distribute dividends in cash. Whether dividends be reinvested or paid out is at the discretion of the funds manager.

Therefore, in order to ensure that you receive exactly what you're anticipating, you should do your homework before choosing a dividend exchange-traded fund.

Exchange-traded funds will eventually get dividend payments in cash since they are required to collect dividends from the companies they own. However, because exchange-traded funds are regarded like stocks, they will be subject to the same dividend-paying deadlines as stocks. This implies that an exchange-traded fund will have a record date and an ex-dividend date that work in the same way as conventional company shares. Stated differently, the purpose of these dates is to ascertain which investors are qualified to receive dividend payments. Every exchange-traded fund with a dividend payment schedule will likewise have a dividend payment date.

An exchange-traded fund, like a firm, will have an investor prospectus. If there are funds that pique your interest,

The money from dividends that exchange-traded funds receive from the other equities in which they are invested is often collected by these funds and placed in a non-interest-bearing account. The funds deposited into the account are held there until the fund has received all of the dividends that are owed to it. After that, it retains them until its payment date, at which point it distributes the funds according to the number of shares you own in the fund and releases the cash.

In fact, some funds approach this differently. They will temporarily invest the money into more shares of stock rather than placing it in a holding account. Then, in order to raise the funds required to distribute the dividends to the investors on the payment date, they will sell those shares. If not, the funds are dispersed in the same manner, with each fund investor receiving a payout that is commensurate with the quantity of stakes they possess.

Furthermore, understanding value investing altered my perspective on money and how to make it. You will also grow increasingly indifferent to the business demand that you exchange your time for money, but at least now you will know what to do and have the means to address it.

Value investing has provided me with access to a wide range of feasible investment opportunities outside of the stock market, as the methods and approaches are not limited to stock buying. This is invaluable knowledge. That's the reason I'm headed towards creating an asset empire that will allow me to escape the confines of a 9–5 work and benefit future generations.

2. Investing with Purpose and Acquiring Expert Knowledge

"Value is what you get, and price is what you pay." Benjamin Graham

Purchasing securities at a substantial discount to their current underlying values and keeping them until a larger portion of their value is realised is known as value investing. The process's key is the element of a bargain. "Seth Klarman."

The idea behind value investing is straightforward:

- Determine the asset's value.
- Buy it for a significant discount on its asking price.
- Watch the price rise until it reaches the asset's value.

This is not the case with conventional investing methods, which assume that value and price are synonymous. Since the market prices goods efficiently, if one share of Apple stock costs $100, its worth must likewise be $100. Undergraduate students studying finance and economics are generally taught this worldview, and almost all of them go on to become Wall Street commentators, brokers, and certified financial advisers.

My primary issue with this market idea is as follows: The future performance of the company is uncertain and will always affect your investment. The price of the stock is significantly impacted by quarterly earnings calls, which provide investors with an overview of the health and wealth of a company.

For instance, Let's say you spent $100 on Apple. At the next earnings call, it's worth $100 as well. Apple's stock price is likely to decline if the company has a dismal quarter. Thus, Apple loses value as a result of it. That's right—you just suffered a financial loss—the ultimate sin of value investing.

Famously, Warren Buffett outlined two essential guidelines for investing:

1. Avoid losing money.

2. Remember rule 1.

When Apple's stock started to decline in value, a Wall Street adherent would probably liquidate their investment before suffering further losses. They conclude that a little upset is preferable to a large loss.

Consider the identical scenario, but swap out the Wall Street drone with a value investor. Although Apple's stock is only $100, the value investor believes it is worth $200. That's because Apple's stock price dropped as a result of the earnings call's bad corporate performance. Outcome? Value investors jump in headfirst.

The stock price drops further, reaching $85. The value investor sees this as a fantastic opportunity to buy rather than sell their investment. Our value investor purchases more stock at $85 with the confidence that the price will soon revert to its inherent worth of $200. He is delighted to have discovered an even better deal on a discounted company.

The stock price reaches $50 as it keeps declining. By then, every analyst on Wall Street had condemned the stock as risky, tradable, and uninvestable. Nevertheless, our value investor has persisted, believing that the price will eventually rise. Throughout, they have been buying additional shares at increasingly attractive discounts.

So, How Is It Done?

Though felling trees is the last thing a sloth would want to do, the former US president's comment highlights the need for thorough planning. It is still true, though, that preparedness is key. Lazy investors should prepare for their investment strategy in this manner.

Investing wisely can result from careful planning.

Step 1: Choose a representative or investment company

If I had to coin a metaphor for this, the money would be the ETFs you purchase, and the investment business would be the wallet.

How, then, do you know where to look for information? It's quite easy. Make use of your copy of the accompanying table: Minimum payment of ($) Cost per month ($)Purchase/sale commissions (%)

Investing Company One Investment Company Two Investment Companies 3.

Now, get in touch with every investment company and pose the following three queries, recording their responses in the table:

How much is the minimum deposit?

What is the monthly Cost of your management fees?

Which commissions do you charge for purchasing and selling securities?

Once finished, your table may resemble this: Minimum payment of ($) Cost per month ($)Purchase/sale commissions (%)

Big-Money Company$5,000.Ten $/0.08%

Money 'n' Sense Purchasing House$10,001 $15,00.7

Brokers Mike M. Rich Associates$10,000 $2,000 0.09%

Thus, if I deposit $1,000 into my Big Money Firm investment account each month and use the whole amount to purchase index ETFs, I will be making monthly payments of $10 + $0.8. This monthly charge may seem high when your portfolio is small. Still, when it reaches the six-figure mark, or over $100,000, the fees you pay seem reasonable and far less expensive than the alternatives, like active funds or continuous property maintenance costs.

After deciding which investment firm to handle your money, you'll need to sign a number of documents and waivers before being able to use the trading system of that company.

You might be delighted when you save money.

While it's true that money cannot buy happiness, having more options and being more independent might help you feel less anxious, depressed, and unsatisfied. Setting and achieving financial goals can also make you feel good, particularly if those goals entail helping others.

You can see what is possible when you save.

Savings are linked to optimistic objectives as well as handling unfavourable situations. However, protection is also tied to managing crises. For instance, you may have always desired to take an art lesson or take a vacation to a different state or nation. Saving helps you see things more for what they could be than for what they are—the world and your life. That kind of thinking is necessary to be strong, inspired, and driven.

REMEMBER: All children ought to be taught how to save. It saves you money, increases your level of independence, and enables you to buy goods that would otherwise be beyond your price range. Usually, it means you have more alternatives or money so that you can accomplish more. It will make you happier as a result. Above all, saving makes you stay focused on your objectives. Establish goals. Examine what is ahead. By conserving money, you can influence events!

HOW ARE MONEY SAVINGS MADE?

Keep money in your bank account.

If you're generating a little money, as young YouTubers like Emily Wass will tell you, you may feel uncomfortable or hesitant to contribute to your savings account. No one anticipates that you will begin working or becoming wealthy when you are a young child. The little money your parents provide you, though, can be saved. If you have a plan and an objective, you can save money for anything, even a tiny purchase of a video game. One way to save money is to deposit it in a bank.

You can ask your parents to open a children's bank account for you if you don't already have one. Establish and adhere to daily, weekly, and monthly savings targets. You may find out how long it will take to reach your goal by using a savings calculator.

After you've established your goals, open a savings account and deposit the funds you plan to save for that duration. This will lessen the temptation to spend money impulsively. Making consistent contributions to your account and staying true to your objectives promotes better spending habits and establishes sound financial management. We shall discuss this in more detail in chapter four.

Author of Common Stocks and Uncommon Profits, Philip Fisher, outlined his strategy for investing in this widely-read book. This involved what he referred to as the "scuttlebutt," or the necessary research an investor has to do on a company's prospects. It could entail speaking with management, a company's vendors, clients, and staff, or simply keeping an eye out for fresh information about the business. Buffett's philosophy that research is never finished and the fact that he had already scuttlebuttedhimself fit this perfectly. The vice president immediately springs to mind when I go up to GEICO's offices on a Saturday as a graduate student. You can also use scuttlebutt. It's a great approach to get further knowledge about your investments.

In addition to disseminating the scuttlebutt, Fisher's masterwork on investing concentrated on the higher-level aspects that Buffett was picking up from Munger. Fisher's book offered a checklist of 15 items to look for while examining a business. Several of them focused on the value of transparent, honest management, while others asked about the company's product line's strength and viability in comparison to its rivals. After being fully persuaded by 1989, Buffett remarked in a letter to shareholders, Purchasing firms with that kind of attitude is stupid unless you are a liquidator. Buffett continued his explanation of why pure cigar butt investing was a bust by describing his encounters with Hochschild-Kohn, the Baltimore department store he and Munger had purchased, which caused them fits.

When he and Munger purchased it, it was as inexpensive as it could get. Decent folks even ran it. However, such outstanding men and women needed to be more sufficient to overcome basic economic incompetence. Buffett and Graham also disagreed on the topic of diversification. Graham has held a number of businesses, but he thinks it's best to concentrate on 2-3. While Graham believes that having a large stock portfolio lowers your risk, he thinks it's a sign that you don't know what you're doing. Therefore, we adopted a strategy that required our being smart (and sometimes, not too smart). Buffett wrote in a 1993 letter to Berkshire shareholders, addressing this point. Thus, a lot of experts argue that the approach has to be riskier than what more traditional investors do. We differ.

Suppose a strategy of portfolio concentration raises, as it should, the degree of comfort an investor needs to feel with a company's economic qualities before investing in it. In that case, it may reduce risk. Using dictionary definitions, we define risk in this opinion as "the possibility of loss or injury." Buffett's investment in GEICO during his graduate studies, following an in-person visit to the company's Washington, D.C., office, exemplifies the divergence in thinking between Buffett and Graham over-diversification. Even though Graham had tiny holdings in numerous businesses, Buffett was already such a strong supporter of GEICO that the young student put three-quarters of his portfolio in the company. Buffett is the epitome of concentration when it comes to stocks. Even while it's vital to take advice from others who have gone before you, feel free to question whether their method is the greatest one available.

Where To Start Investing And How

Investing only requires a few button clicks. Your brokerage account can be opened in a matter of seconds, and if you employ electronic fund transfers, the report can be funded as well. There is a procedure that you must adhere to. It will also be necessary for you to find a reliable broker.

USA's Top Broker Firms

A dependable broker is essential if you plan to begin investing. Since brokers are subject to strict regulations in the stock market, all you really need to know is who the biggest names in the business are and what kind of account they demand in order to open one you can pick the broker of your choice.

Below is a list of the best brokerage houses:

Defender

By Scottrade

Buy Sell

Trade America

Schwab Charles

Honesty

Jones, Edward

When it comes to managing personal accounts, some of these companies provide more than others. All statements, regardless of size, are eligible for individual account managers from Edward Jones, Fidelity, and Charles Schwab. They enable you to monitor your account, get an account overview and investing recommendations, and deposit money into accounts like stocks or mutual funds. Long-term investments are better suited for these three companies.

For day traders, there is E-Trade, Scottrade, Ameritrade, and Vanguard. These businesses provide an online trading platform where you may view all stocks, mutual funds, and other goods that can be traded. In addition, these four organizations do not assign a personal account manager to every account; instead, they provide tutorials, education programmes, forums, help buttons, and a variety of customer assistance options. It is assumed that you wish to execute trades independently, manage deals, and hold both long and short positions. Compared to retirement investors, it is more for day traders and less for retirees.

Analysis, both technical and fundamental

It will be necessary for you to do both technical and fundamental analysis when it comes to the particular equities you choose to purchase. For instance, just because you might not be considering penny stocks, in the long run, doesn't mean you shouldn't conduct the same kind of research on them as you would on other companies.

Looking at the firm itself—its earnings, the state of the economy, its financial operations, and the company's financials—as well as keeping a watch on facts pertaining to the particular company itself constitute fundamental analysis. This is a more significant and long-term issue to consider while developing your strategy. When investing in penny stocks, it is still a good idea to be informed about the company's operations. It may not be necessary for you to concentrate as much on the far future.

Technical analysis is primarily concerned with stock charts, trending data, and other technical aspects related to the financial performance of the company, particularly with respect to its shares. Before you start investing in penny stocks, it's crucial that you comprehend the entire extent of this key skill that you will need to learn.

Looking to Trade Stocks

your situation, or the company you want to invest in. As a result, it's critical to hone your skills in a simulation to determine what you are comfortable with and to gain a general understanding of what you are doing. You might concentrate on adhering to the following rules to aid you:

You might concentrate on conducting pre-market research first. This is the place to identify stocks that meet your exact requirements even before the market starts on that particular day.

Second, it's critical to keep an eye out for "gappers," or instances in which the organization is experiencing a significant event, such as the revelation of huge news. When a stock meets all the conditions for trading but is trading at a lower price than you had anticipated, it is said to be gapping.

Thirdly, you must possess a solid grasp of chart patterns. This is where learning maths in school paid off because you will now need to develop your close reading skills. Numerous tactics depend on analyzing the candlestick chart, and it's important to recognize when an upward or downward trend is occurring.

Given the speculative nature of the data, numerous assumptions must be made. Nonetheless, you can create rather strong and accurate instructions for the long hall if you practise these techniques effectively. This is particularly useful if you see patterns or objects like bull flags. This typically identifies things like risk points and serves as an excellent predictor of when to exit a particular transaction.

It would be best if you become accustomed to speculating because penny stock trading mostly requires an understanding of behavioural factors and the ability to recognize trends.

Changing Out of out-of-date technology

Investors are among the many who believe that virtual and augmented reality will quickly replace existing methods. In the past, this has yet to occur. New technology is "additive" at first, gradually displacing those earlier forms. We heard about this.

A radio show could only be listened to on a physical radio at first. However, radio shows could be heard online in the early days of the internet. It was made available online as an additional means of listening to the same radio programme that was carried on AM or FM stations. Then, over time, we began to receive radio programmes that were exclusively accessible online. This gave rise to podcasts, and today, a whole generation only listens to long-form audio content on podcasts. It is a significant change that occurred gradually.

The Travis Scott performance on Fortnite and the Little Nas X concert on Roblox are two more examples of this from the present. These performers aren't replacing traditional shows; rather, they're adding them as a means of interaction with their followers and a chance for them to listen to their music. In this way, a lot of our current routines will gradually spread into virtual environments.

Virtual reality types
Virtual reality comes in a plethora of varieties. The term "virtual reality" is frequently employed in marketing to promote interactive video games, TV shows, and 3D films. However, as none of them completely immerse you in a virtual or partially virtual world, none of

them can be considered virtual realities. You won't get the necessary experience from all of virtual reality.

The totally absorbing virtual environment

Let's say you would like to experience everything in virtual reality. If that's the case, you ought to possess a device that allows you to engage with this intricate virtual environment, and the computer ought to be able to recognize everything that happens and even customize your experience every time. Your computer's hardware must allow you to walk around in the virtual environment completely. You will want two screens and a head-mounted display with stereo sound if you wish to enjoy these virtual realities fully. You'll want to put on a pair or two of sensory gloves. A loudspeaker surrounds you so that the visuals are projected from the outside, and you are free to roam about the space.

Chapter 9: Novel Initiative and Prospects - An Example of Instagram

Mark Zuckerberg, the CEO of Facebook, declared that the company would start trading as "meta platforms" on December 1. Rather than being a social media platform, he would rather see Facebook Media transform into a metaverse firm.

Facebook has started making significant investments in augmented and virtual reality. They have been developing a world for virtual reality called Horizon, which may be explored with a quest headset they manufacture. Facebook rebranded itself as "meta platforms Inc." on November 1, indicating their aspiration for the Metaverse to become a reality and their expectation that the Metaverse will eventually replace Facebook.

The concept of a virtual platform that may be accessed by several individuals using different devices is known as the meta-universe. They can travel around the virtual environment, engage in social interaction, have fun, and explore. Many businesses were already working on bringing the Metaverse to life before

Mark Zuckerberg declared that he would like to be part of building this imagined future. They were creating a wide range of technology and software that would be used for the Metaverse. The development of the Metaverse will require time and the unwavering support of our current tech giants.

Many developers and entrepreneurs will benefit from the creation of a metaverse by having the opportunity to market their goods in the form of non-fungible tokens.

Technique 9: Market Lemonade

This is a fantastic summertime side gig for earning extra cash. The ideal course of action is to get your parents' assistance in setting up a small lemonade stand next to a busy location with plenty of workers, such as a construction site. Make sure you have enough lemonade for at least four or five litres. This will be a much-needed refreshment if it's a hot day and many people are working on the site. I'll provide a tried-and-true lemonade recipe that is sure to please.

components for making homemade lemonade

Two cups of freshly squeezed lemon juice (bottled juice is also OK)

Five-litre cold water

A quarter of a cup of sugar

slices of lemons to embellish

Try two tablespoons of table salt.

Freeze

Steps to Make Your Lemonade: Parents can assist you!

Step 1: Combine the sugar, lemon juice, water, and salt in a big pitcher and stir until the sugar dissolves.

Step 2: Garnish with lemon wedges.

Step 3: Transport this to the desired selling location in containers.

Step 3: To keep the beverage cold, add ice last.

It's time to set up your stand and start selling your lemonade.

● Find out where you can obtain authorization to run a lemonade stand. Lemonade of sale may require you to abide by stringent zoning laws in some locations. Permission is likely needed before you can begin selling lemonade. To be sure you're following the rules of lemonade stands, check with your town.

See if your parents can get assistance from your city council in finding out. Go online and check the town or city website to find out if lemonade booths are subject to any local rules.

Select locations where there is a lot of foot traffic to stand out. A walkway may be found next to a large grocery store, at a busy crossroads, or near a sporting event. On hot, sunny days, customers are more likely to want to buy your lemonade since they might be thirsty and want a refreshing beverage. Choose a busy area.

Verify whether it is permissible to erect a kiosk outside of a structure or store. To find out if you can make lemonade and sell it on that corner, you need to talk to the management.

As it provides you with a greater chance to obtain more resources, set up outside your front yard. If your house is close by, put up a lemonade stand on a road with some traffic. Some of the products you'll need to replenish your inventory can be found in your residence. To make your clients' lemonade even more refreshing, you can keep ice and lemonade in your refrigerator. It also makes it easier for an adult to keep an eye on you and your posture, which will keep you safe.

● Select an area with some shade to force people to take breaks. People are far more likely to buy cool lemonade in or near shaded areas. On bright, sunny days, when the coolness is most pleasant, shady locations look their best. Think about where you could place your stand and how you could shield the sun. Go to a nearby park if it's allowed so you can sell to lots of people there. Because there are so many people in parks, it's a great idea to sell plenty of lemonade to thirsty people and kids running around. As long as it's allowed, pick a location close to a well-trafficked park or play area to draw clients before you even open.

● To encourage customers to pull over, position your stand where it is visible from the street. Making sure your lemonade stand is visible to passing motorists is important since you never know when a driver may need a place to park and shop. Orient your table and display it so that people riding bicycles, strolling, or driving can see it.

Your supplier costs assist you in determining the price. Determine how much you invested in your stand first, and then think about how much you hope to make. Add up all of the money you've spent on your perspective, including the cost of the signs you made and the lemons and lemonade powder you purchased.

Let's take an example where you start your lemonade stand with $10. To break even, you would need to sell 20 glasses of lemonade if you were to charge 50 cents a cup. Adding up your costs will allow you to determine your earnings from selling lemonade. You should budget between 50 cents and $1 for a glass of lemonade.

Employing a Financial Advisor

It can be challenging to find time for your money if you are employed in the financial sector. Furthermore, having access to a variety of financial options and techniques can be perplexing. The majority of people need more time and expertise to become financial experts. For this reason, there are financial advisors. Financial advisors are professionals in their area who assist clients with matters pertaining to personal finance and asset management. They are able to assemble a complete investment portfolio and savings plan for you.

Getting a planner could be the best course of action for you if you need more assistance and feel stressed out about your money. Just do some research; there are lots of excellent specialists out there. But proceed with extreme caution. The field of financial advising is unregulated. This implies that practically anyone can identify oneself as a financial counsellor by hanging a sign on their door. Seek out those who have professional credentials, such as a license as a certified financial planner. Get referrals and reviews on specific individuals as well. Never follow someone unthinkingly just because they seem like an authority. Recall that hiring a financial planner will also cost money. Choose the most suitable candidate for your specific requirements. Before you hire someone, make sure to ask them these questions.

Have you worked with clientele similar to mine before?

What will the cost be? Will the investments I make bring in money for you?

When will we get together to talk about our financial goals?

How frequently can I get in touch with you? Are there any restrictions?

Remember that there are numerous ways to get in touch with a financial planner, thanks to modern technology and communication techniques. It's optional for you to collaborate with locals. Just make sure there are other ways to access them easily. Verify if hiring a financial planner would be worthwhile, and anticipate a long-term partnership. A lot of financial planners provide consultations at no cost. Use these to your advantage and schedule meetings with multiple people before deciding. Since it is your money, you have the right.

This chapter's goal was to familiarise you with one of the safest ways to enter the world of finance. If you want more long-term growth out of your money than what a standard savings or checking account can offer, passive investment funds are a reliable option. Though the risk is by no means nil, it is rather minimal compared to more actively managed funds in terms of the possibility of suffering significant losses or filing for bankruptcy.

4.4% What role do cryptocurrencies play?

This digital currency is widely used in the e-commerce industry as one of the most popular means of transacting. It's imperative to accept bitcoin payments while interacting with an online retailer.

secure exchange

It has long been a source of frustration for both consumers and retailers to complete a safe and secure transaction in exchange for their goods. Because they fear that the credit card information they provide online may be fake or fraudulent, people are hesitant to make purchases from online retailers. But, cryptocurrencies have found a solution to this problem.

The only thing that allows a holder to spend or convert money is their private key. It is only useful to have a holder with a key.

Another wonderful feature of Bitcoin that improves security is its "wallet" feature. A wallet's unique identification can be used to determine who is temporarily in possession of it. Walletcontaining units have a lower chance of being stolen.

Blockchain technology makes data manipulation impossible. This approach can detect even the smallest modifications in encryption. Since the source code determines the amount of units in the world, there is no way to create a cryptocurrency. Furthermore, once a transfer is executed, it cannot be reversed, evading fraud protection.

Recognizing businesses and protecting data.

Users of the internet have been concerned about their privacy ever since it first became available. Anonymity was the most satisfying feature back then. But the development of technology erased such mystery. Supporters of Bitcoin have long placed a high value on anonymity and privacy.

When your website is prepared to accept Bitcoin payments, you will be able to assist customers who would rather not be followed by people or organizations. Anyone looking to steer clear of such issues is more likely to choose a business that accepts cryptocurrencies.

Taking cryptocurrency payments for your online store could help you become the best in your industry or build brand awareness for your business.

As more and more laws requiring monitoring are put into place, people are increasing the effort they put into remaining unknown. Since you can reach them and engage with them on a deeper level using a cryptocurrency payment system, you'll be able to communicate with these people and persuade them to make purchases at your online business.

Delocalization

The fact that cryptocurrencies are decentralized is advantageous to both consumers and retailers.

Unlike their real equivalents, virtual currencies are not affiliated with any one organization or government. No one can claim it, nor can anyone exert any effect over it.

Cryptocurrencies offer a reliable means of currency exchange that is unrestricted by national banks. You don't have to be concerned about different laws that might be legal in one country but a major barrier in another. Decentralization may be especially tempting to people who are worried about the consequences of quantitative easing and other loose monetary policies.

Owners of e-commerce businesses run a genuine risk of losing their assets and bank accounts due to political unrest. However, this isn't possible with cryptocurrencies because of their decentralized structure. When needed, cash can be retrieved from a number of locations worldwide.

Guidelines to Follow

First of all, the holy grail does not exist. Whether an expert writes a best-selling book telling you to buy a stock when its price is above the 50-period moving average and guarantees you never lose money is irrelevant. It is more complicated. Try as you would; you cannot account for all the other factors that need to be taken into account when considering a company.

Does this imply that value investment is worthless? Naturally not. While there isn't a magic bullet that will guarantee success every time, there is a method that, when adhered to diligently, will eventually provide results. You will gain a great deal of arsenal-worthy weaponry from this book that will help you win. However, you will have complete control over how you use them.

Once more, investing is neither formulaic nor predictable, and you should not listen to anyone who promises you will get rich quickly. Consider this: If the product or service they are endorsing were always effective for everyone, then there would be no market since everyone would be acting in the same way. The stock price trend is fixed. It's not true, as stated.

Carry out your research. That is not a choice. Visit a casino if you wish to gamble. To determine a company's worth, you have to be prepared to do extensive maths. You have access to materials that can assist you with this, but it does not absolve you of responsibility for comprehending the ramifications and interpreting the results. You ought to be prepared to examine every detail regarding a business, including potential worth and the correlation between market value and price.

You need to exercise discipline, as you will discover if you look past the obvious in the previous paragraph. This cannot be avoided. After doing the necessary research and analysis and making the best use of the appropriate metrics, you must be prepared to either wait patiently if necessary or act quickly to seize the opportunity when the ideal price for you arises.

It would be prudent for you as a value investor to constantly check for stability in the firm you're examining's earnings, returns, asset value, supplier chain, and client base. You want the same level of consistency that you would get if you ordered your preferred coffee at Starbucks.

The last thing you need is even the slightest ambiguity, which is why consistency is important. Uncertainty indicates the presence of risk. You will require a larger amount of funds for your venture when there is a risk. You make the decision that you don't even want to work for that company since you know that other investors are probably just as nervous as you are and could leave at any time. Hence, aim for consistency when making investments to reduce risk and boost your margin of safety. However, this does not imply that value investment is risk-free. All you need to do is ensure that your rewards are not equal to your risk. You have to focus just on consistent and dependable performance.

Be mindful of the intangible. We are discussing topics such as branding and client loyalty. These are equally significant to the numbers. These things are important because they have an impact on the figures. You should be aware of the state of the market, the products, how consumers and the general public see the product, how customers respond to it, opinions, the supply chain, leadership, and all these other intangibles.

It matters to have a safety margin. Once more, value investing is purchasing your business for a price that feels extremely low to you, giving you a buffer of safety. In this manner, you will be covered in the event that things don't turn out the way you had anticipated—which they rarely do. In addition to looking for a deal, you should also look for margins of safety within the business you are evaluating, such as moats or competitive advantages that separate it from the competition. An additional safeguard is if the company has a lot of cash on hand or is debt-free.

Don't bother with diversity. While diversification has its merits, value investing suffers from diluted rewards due to diversification. The secret is to select the best-value companies. There's no need to diversify if you're doing things correctly. There's always a chance that you're throwing away much too much money when you diversify too much. Although you could diversify at first, you'd be better off cutting it down as you improve.

Stir it. Investing in value is not a zero-sum game. It can be applied to around 85–90% of your stock portfolio. Just be sure to choose carefully and be ready for this to be a long-term issue. However, don't hesitate to employ some aggressive options in the near future. For example, you may purchase call options.

It Is Not Investing in Wholesale

Wholesaling is one of the most well-known land-contributing schemes offered to unskilled investors. In wholesaling, as the distributor, you find incredible deals on speculation and provide them to investors. You then make money by charging the investor more than you originally agreed upon. For example, you see a house going for $50,000, and you see yourself as a flipper willing to spend $55,000 for it. You retain the difference between the two costs—your profit—by handling the administrative tasks and acting as the middleman.

Seems very easy enough.

There are numerous benefits to wholesaling. Amazing real estate investing skills like math, deal-finding, negotiation, and networking may be learned from it. Additionally, it costs very little or nothing to start so that everyone can do it. It might even be satisfying. Wholesaling is a really easy activity that you can perform alone and with whatever level of creativity you need to put into it, even though it's not always as easy to enter into as it's frequently made out to be.

Here's the harsh reality, though. The promotion of wholesaling is akin to that of speculative methods. Not in the slightest is selling a speculative methodology wholesale. Wholesale of sale is all labour and no speculation. Even though you might have spent some money creating your flyers or advertising materials, it is still relevant to your wholesaling firm.

Selling wholesale requires labour. If you decide to start wholesaling, you've accepted a task. It's perfectly acceptable to take on a new role as long as it's one you intend to

take up. In the near future, you will typically have the option to create cycles and frameworks for your wholesaling business and hire people to complete the tasks on your behalf in order to make it appear less of a labour-intensive undertaking, but all of that still involves work. It's keeping up a company. If you currently work 60 hours a week, are the head of a team of five, and need to start contributing, you should definitely pursue that. If you decide against it, you might be better off taking on a second job than contributing, but that might not be feasible given your hectic schedule.

While wholesaling can be a great way to generate capital to invest in real estate and teach you a lot about contributing, you can also generate money by taking on additional work, obtaining loans, selling goods on eBay, or starting a different kind of business—activities that might be more appealing to you than wholesaling. I would rather not demolish the myth that wholesaling is the easiest way for someone without money to start making a difference, even though it isn't.

Chapter 7: Swing Trading Foundations

An additional strategy used by investors to optimize returns is swing trading. Due to the longer time horizon that investors are aiming for, this strategy requires greater patience. Swing trading, therefore, extends beyond day trading's one-day time span. Swing trading involves investors holding open positions for a few days to several weeks at a time.

Since we're looking at a longer time frame, we're anticipating significantly larger swings in price activity, which is the main goal of swing trading. We're looking for considerably bigger swings in price action rather than price action that moves in cents. Hundreds or even thousands of dollars could be involved, depending on the size of the post.

What Separates Swing Trading From Day Trading

Day trading and swing trading function similarly overall. There is usage of the same kind of trading platform. Additionally, the same methods and analytical resources are applied. The time range in which deals are placed is the primary distinction.

The application of risk/reward ratios is another significant distinction. A risk/reward ratio is predicated on the difference between possible gains and losses. Naturally, a transaction is worthwhile to enter if the gain justifies the cost. A risk-to-benefit ratio of 3:1, for example, is a reasonable general rule of thumb. Stated differently, you are taking a $1 risk in exchange for a $3 profit. Risk-to-reward ratios don't really apply to day trading because the trades are so brief.

It's important to note that swing trading calls for patience. You must be prepared to wait for market fluctuations to happen. They are incredibly erratic. As a result, you must be ready to hold off until you achieve the price points that you want. If not, close the deal before the target price is reached.

In this context, price, volatility, and volume are all relevant. You can base your selections on the objective data provided by these indicators. You're not making irrational investment decisions as a result.

The study of non-quantitative elements influencing price behaviour is known as fundamental analysis. These primarily consist of political, economic, and—above all—psychological aspects. When examining a long-term picture, fundamental analysis is crucial. For instance, investors' perspectives are influenced by government political decisions. As a result, investors may decide to stay away from the market if they start to feel nervous about possible changes in it. On the other hand, investors might enter the race if things appear promising. Therefore, the key to any effective swing trading technique is a thorough understanding of fundamental analysis.

In order to succeed in swing trading, you must educate yourself in both technical and fundamental analysis. As such, swing trading necessitates a higher time and effort commitment. The state of the market is something you must closely monitor. You will be able to anticipate opportunities as a result. If you can accurately predict future swings, you can benefit handsomely.

Earnings Per Share (EPS): During an earnings report, EPS is typically one of the first to be released. Because EPS indicates a company's earnings per share, and a higher EPS means a stock has a better value when compared to others in its industry, this creates an immediate shift in the price of the store. A high EPS suggests that dividend payments to shareholders may be imminent for the corporation. It can be used to demonstrate a company's profitability as well as its lack thereof.

Remember that the EPS is more of a snapshot of short-term activity and a cursory look at profitability than it is a comprehensive assessment of the company's success.

Dividend Yield: The portion of the company's profit that is allocated to shareholders is known as the dividend. Established corporations such as Johnson & Johnson and Coca-Cola have managed to generate profits over time, allowing them to distribute their extra shares to their shareholders. Since growth stocks are still in their infancy, they will not pay dividends. Due to the passive income flow generated by dividend investment, value investors and high-net-worth individuals are the ideal candidates.

Example of a Coca-Cola dividend

With a $1,000,000 investment in Coca-Cola, which yields a 3% annual yield, you can anticipate receiving $30,000 in dividend payments each year. Since dividends are typically paid every three months, you will receive $7,500 in earnings each quarter (excluding capital gains). Over the last five years, Coca-Cola's stock price has increased by thirty per cent. Your $1,000,000 investment would now be worth $1,300,000, and you would receive a 3% payment on the $1,300,000 current value. The amount of your dividend has grown to $39,000 from $30,000. Depending on their circumstances, companies may also decide to raise or lower rewards. This is a very efficient method of generating passive income, but it works best for asset preservation rather than portfolio growth.

Total Addressable Market: This industry's total income is available. This is significant because it demonstrates the entire potential of the industry and the company going forward. Software, for instance, has no bounds since it can keep innovating and generating revenue from its current user base.

Facebook Case Study

Facebook boasts an incredible user base that continues to increase every day. Even though they have a niche in the social industry, advertising accounts for the majority of their revenue. Thanks to software's great flexibility, businesses can make money anywhere. Purchasing new companies enables them to grow as well.

Example of Gaming

The gaming industry is one example of a sector that may be capped since, despite having a sizable audience, it is only able to reach some. It is relatively small in comparison to other significant worldwide industries. As of right now, the global social gaming market is estimated to be worth 79 billion dollars, and by 2024, it is projected to grow to 99 billion dollars. Thus, although this industry is obviously expanding, its scope still needs to be developed. Apple is a part of the mobility business, which has a TAM of $10 trillion.

It's your time now. Create an Excel spreadsheet, enter the stock information, and start your investigation. Recall that every successful business started as a tiny one and grew over time. Hence, it would be best if you exercised patience while making investments and resist the urge to sell when market cycles frighten you. These are the greatest chances to purchase and gain more ownership at a lower cost.

Chapter 3: Investing versus Winning

Stock trading and investing are two distinct activities. "I put money into it. I invest in stocks." Day trading stocks eventually turns into gambling instead of investing. When will that happen?
"Investing" is defined as "TO MAKE A FINANCIAL COMMITMENT IN ORDER TO GET A RETURN" in the Miriam Webster Dictionary, whereas "gambling" is described as "THE PRACTISE OR ACTION OF BETTING." These have a similar tone.

Your client may relate their employment to that of a Wall Street brokerage business or bank "trader"—"a person who sells and buys things, currencies, or stocks," according to the dictionary—depending on their level of experience.

Now that these words are starting to sound so similar, let's exercise some common sense.

Is it expected that the money will be given back immediately?

Most stock investors expect a dividend while they wait for a steady increase in value. If you go to a casino and play slots, blackjack, or roulette, you know your results instantly. If the plan calls for buying and holding, it's usually investing; if you want your money back immediately, usually before settlement day, it's gambling.

Are you sure that this is what you want to do?

Economics is the foundation of investing. Technical factors also come into play. Certain strategies, like margin trading or buying options, take a lot of work to learn. If you put money down and you know the risks involved, you are investing. If you put money down and you don't see how the outcome will be achieved, you are gambling.

Does this stock have a strong cause to rise?

Typically, investors buy stocks based on earnings. They know that a store must perform well; buying without a good reason to think it will increase in value is gambling. The stock will rise as a result of the company's efforts, which will increase sales, profits, and earnings.

Do you make unaffordable purchases with money?

The vast majority of the funds are secure; gamblers are those who waste their petrol money and toll money in a casino. Investors make financial commitments based on the Investment Pyramid. Investors are aware of the risk and make decisions based on that information.

Are you guided by research or your gut?

Investors recognize trends, have reason to believe a notion will flourish, and gamblers anticipate hitting it rich.

Investors frequently conduct fundamental studies to find hidden jewels that others have missed.

Does losing all of your money pose a risk to you?

Investors diversify their portfolios to minimize their losses; if you lose at roulette, blackjack, or slots, you won't be paid for that hand or spin. They set and adhere to downside restrictions. Investors seldom put themselves in a situation where they have to be all or nothing.

Do you commit to a project "all in"?

Do you invest all of your money in one endeavour, or do you spread it out? Gamblers are prepared to risk everything in the hopes of striking it lucky.

Furthermore, even though everyone is affected, the people most negatively impacted by expansion are those with fixed incomes; if you were expecting to need a certain amount of venture capital on which you could eventually quit, development would require that amount to be much higher. More cash pursuing a similar measure of labour and products has the immediate circumstances and logical results of driving up costs (because of the depreciation of the dollar).

The number you should have should increase with expansion. If you're wondering if there's a way to offset the negative effects of development, the answer is definitely yes. Still, it doesn't include investing in gold and silver or stocks, bonds, mutual funds, or any other financial instrument.

Think about our seniors, those 65 years of age and older, who are typically not presently successfully obtaining compensation or working in organizations. Their "dynamic" pay has ceased, and they are dependent upon retirement plans, Social Security, and their venture savings. How does all of this really affect you and me?

As they should, most seniors are moderate financial backers. It is important to protect the corpus or head venture capital. They need be in a position to take on risky investments where the chief could lose out. Younger people can make up for such losses, but after age 62, time is of the essence.

Seniors, on the other hand, put their money into low-risk investments like money market accounts, savings accounts, and bank certificates of deposit, which yield less than a 2% return, leaving little to offset increases in health care, prescription drug costs, and living expenses. Put another way, our government's reckless fiscal policies and monetary policies are hurting seniors the most when they can least afford it.

There is a method that the innovative movement of people just like you and me could provide some intervention for the good of our seniors.

Savings accounts, money market accounts, and bank CDs are examples of relatively conservative investments that allowed savers to prosper in the past. However, due to the Federal Reserve's control over financing costs, savers—the majority of whom are seniors and retired—are facing serious difficulties today. Profits from moderate ventures are currently in the low single digits; after representing charges and expansion, such a low return cannot provide the income necessary to maintain the standard of living for most. As a result, many should attack the head of their retirement speculations, cut back on their lifestyle, and take on part-time or full-time employment.

To their hardship, they paid attention to all-around implied appeal from the people who had depended on more traditional monetary and retirement models, which don't work today. Moderate saving and speculation is not a practical plan. This was not the vision of people in this persevering age when they thought they had arranged and saved well.

Why Excellent Chances Are Seldom Found

Most inexperienced investors examine the number of dips and gains in a stock's price chart. They believe they could have made a significant amount of money if they had entered the market before a decline and left at the top. However, it takes a lot of work to do this in the real world. The short-term price activity of the market is unpredictable, making it very difficult to forecast.

This is the reason why short-term tactics like day trading are ineffective. To create money, you have to seek excellent possibilities continuously, and doing so can be challenging. Great opportunities come along infrequently in real life. Why would the stock market be any different?

Consider the number of enormous opportunities you have had in your life that have the potential to change your life or have already done so. You'll notice that chances like these only arise once every ten years or less. Unusual events happen because they are uncommon; otherwise, they wouldn't be considered remarkable. As a result, you shouldn't anticipate seeing them frequently in the stock market.

How Much to Invest?

Getting a respectable return for the level of risk you take on is the fundamental goal of investing. Purchasing the appropriate tool is how you construct these circumstances. I do not mean to refer to stocks, FX, or commodities as instruments. Rather, I'm discussing the relative importance of assets and liabilities and how to invest in as many assets as you can while reducing your liabilities.

Anything that generates cash flow and has worth is considered an asset. The cash flow point is crucial because it provides a basis for analysis and quantification. For example, although gold is frequently recommended as an excellent investment, it is not an asset because it generates no cash flow. Its worth is contingent upon the opinions of others. It would become worthless if everyone decided today that mud and gold are the same thing.

Well, bitcoin is similar to other cryptocurrencies. It generates no cash flow, is irrelevant in the real world save from a few aspirations, and fluctuates by more than 10% the moment a billionaire tweets about it. As a result, the only factor that determines its value is what other people believe.

Your investment in these speculative products (gold or bitcoin) is risky. Being speculative is perfectly acceptable, but it's crucial to remember that these aren't investments. Assets are a part of investments, and one can measure the performance of assets.

Conversely, a liability is anything that depletes value. An automobile, for example, is a burden since it accrues interest on vehicle loans, and its value steadily decreases. Liabilities, however, are not fixed, and under certain situations, they can become assets. Your car is a benefit if you need it to work or conduct business. The money you make more than makes up for any interest you pay.

In the same way, a mortgaged home that doesn't cover your rent is a burden. In the hopes that it may eventually be worth more than you paid for it, you incur maintenance fees and pay interest. To put it briefly, you need other people to think it's worth more than it is right now.

It also helps you with partially or fully paying your mortgage. Because of this, it's an asset that improves the quality of your cash flow and most likely doesn't cause you any financial hardship.

Another notable thing about assets is that, because of the value they create, they are nearly always worth more in the future than they are now. An excellent illustration of this is an internet firm, which has both clients and cash flow and can appreciate over time as long as it continues to generate revenue. Considering the value of those projected cash flows, it makes sense to invest in it.

Gaining an understanding of the distinctions between assets and liabilities is essential to being a successful investor. Generally speaking, anything that puts a strain on your cash flow can be considered speculative or a liability. An asset and an investment is something that increases it or keeps it constant.

Keep in mind that wise speculation can yield profits. It's challenging to execute, though, for the reasons I've already discussed.

Qualities Of A Successful Business?

Introducing

Is it easy to find a good long-term business? If you glance at history, you will notice that very few companies manage to endure over time. Make a list, for instance, of companies that have failed or gone bankrupt in the last 20 years. (Examples: Countrywide Mortgages, Enron, Chrysler, Delta Airlines, and Lehman Brothers.) Why do you believe that certain businesses succeed while others fail? How can we distinguish the winners for investing purposes from the losers?

HOW CAN I DETERMINE IF A BUSINESS IS SUITABLE?

Assume that we have two friends who plan to open modest businesses. First friend, Jack, wants to start a chain of candy stores called "Jack's Candy Shop." He will spend $2,000 building it, and each will bring in $1,000 annually in profits. A whopping 50% return on investment is that! ($1,000/$2,000) as (ROI) He will have made his $2,000 investment back in two years. He would have doubled his money in four years if the stores continued to be profitable at $1,000 annually. This is undoubtedly a pretty incredible business.

Now, Jill, our other friend, wants to start a chain of specialty pet stores called "Just Rodontits." Additionally, building a store costs $2,000, but it's a bad business decision—after all, who wants to own a pet rat? Furthermore, it only generates $40 in profits annually, or a 2% return on investment. ($2,000/$40) The cost to build both stores is the same, but one makes more money than the other.

The owners approach you with the possibility of investing $1,000 each to purchase half of their respective stores. Do you own any investments in Jill's Rodent Shop or Jack's Candy Shop? Naturally, the solution is clear: you choose the business with a larger return (50% in this example).

The best businesses are always those that generate a high return on capital, also known as return on equity or ROE for short. Consider the return on equity (ROE) that a company provides to you as a shareholder each year. It's the distinction between getting a $20 bill or a $10 statement every year. A 20% return on equity (ROE) is superior to a 10% ROE, and Jack's 50% return on capital is exceptional. Therefore, is a business that consistently earns a higher return on equity (ROE) every day worth more than one that does not? Not invariably.

Consider this example: Which would you prefer: 20 dollars every day followed by 10 dollars every day for the remainder of your life, or $15 dollars every day followed by $15 dollars every day for the remainder of your life?

Response: You'd definitely want to live off of $15 for the remainder of your life. (In case you were wondering, the difference is that you will receive $350k for the $15 per day and $233k for the $10 per day).

2.3. Cash's "Fatal Flaw"

The most obvious flaw in Cash isn't that it is unknown; rather, that is its tragic defect. It's not so much that losers use it as it is by real con artists who obtain financial authorization and con large numbers of people. Anyone can access it without having to review it. Cash is a distributed value system that is open, clear-cut, movable, and obvious.

However, the most notable drawback is that topography and area impose obligations on it. It requires greater scope and reach.

We now have access to a different kind of digital currency, which is distributed, conditional, open, unambiguous, and movable. However, this one can be used even when your government forbids you from doing so because it is neutral, unforgeable, borderless, and resistant to censorship. Character or advantage are not necessary. Anyone, anywhere in the world, could use it by simply downloading the product onto whichever processing device they choose. That is the real grievance at hand. We have our special little talks in wealthy countries about who should manage digital currencies, how much we should control them, and whether we should control cryptographic forms of money, but... Screw that! Whether we like them or not, digital currencies are associated with providing universal access to vital funds to anyone who needs them, anywhere in the world.

With universal basic money, what will people do? They will act in the same manner that they have provided financial assistance to millennia. They'll make up a future for their kids.

2.3.1. The Fear Politics

We are paralyzed with fear due to a few troublemakers, unaware that the majority of incredibly bad performers have the advantage and support of the state, that they are inextricably linked to knowledge organizations, and that they are part of the tools of free enterprise observation. With our assessment money, to the tune of trillions of dollars, they reserve despots and drug lords from one end of the world to the other.

Real psychological oppression and drug financing happens not with pennies on the dollar or in cryptocurrency, but rather with barrels of oil and US dollar wire transfers, orchestrated by banks that keep getting bailed out. They will disregard the enormous number of passings they have contributed to and pay a fine that barely warrants a portion of their benefit. Not one person is imprisoned alone.

Some people are brave enough to suggest that we should abolish money in order to put an end to wrongdoing. How profoundly impacted. About 18% of people in the US do not use banking administration services. That only amounts to 60 million individuals.

A financial controller in the back once raised their hand in response to my presentation of this reality during a financial meeting, asking, "Why should we give ledgers to illegals?"

Although that is a frightening question to ask, allow me to explain it to you in a way that will impact you more: "Those people don't deserve the benefit of financial inclusion."

You might laugh out loud when your neighbour remarks, "Those people don't belong in our neighbourhood." All of a sudden, you realize that you are living next to an extremist. However, in my cool response to this banking regulator's question, "Why should we give bank accounts to illegals," I said. Yes, we will. (People aren't "illegals" or illicit either.)

fluctuations in the markets

As the years and decades pass, investors can reasonably rely on long-term trends in the stock market, but in the short term, the market is very volatile. That means that, over brief periods, prices vary up and down. Those who invest for the long time tend to ignore volatility. This explains why proponents of conservative investing methods will frequently advise consumers to utilize dollar-cost averaging. This results in an average of the market's volatility. By purchasing shares when the price is a little lower than it should be, you'll balance out any mistakes you make in buying stocks when the price is a little higher than it should be.

In a way, the stock market is a chaotic system in the short run. Therefore, you can only be certain of what the stock price will be tomorrow or the day after that if there is something specific on offer, such as Apple releasing a new device that investors believe will be a big hit. A rise in one day does not necessarily indicate that there will be more; there could be a notable decline the next day.

For instance, the price of Apple's stock had dropped as low as $196 the Friday before I was writing this. It fluctuated in value over the next few days, closing at $203 on the most recent close. The movements over a brief period seem random. The true course that Apple is taking is only apparent in the long run.

Naturally, Apple is coming to the end of a ten-year journey that started with the release of the iPhone and iPad. Even though call options are a good long-term investment, it's a fair bet that the stock will need to move more to allow for profitable short-term trades; additionally, the price per share is relatively high.

The truth is that a trader who purchases call options actually benefits from volatility. However, volatility can be a friend, but it can also get you into serious trouble. So, be cautious when around it.

More volatile stocks are an options trader's friend because the trader is engaging in a game of probability. Stated differently, what you're searching for are stocks that have the potential to outperform the strike price that will allow you to profit. Large movements in a volatile stock increase the likelihood that it will not only pass your strike price but also do so in a way that significantly exceeds it, giving you the opportunity to profit handsomely.

Naturally, there is also the chance that the stock price will plummet out of the blue. Care must, therefore, be a part of your trader's toolbox. A volatile stock has the same chance of dropping sharply in value as it does of soaring past your strike price.

Moreover, while you're a beginner and might get caught with your pants down, volatile stocks are going to attract experienced options traders. That means that the stock will be in high demand when it comes to options contracts. What happens when there is a high demand for something? The price shoots up. In the case of call options, that means the stock will come with a higher premium. You will need to take the higher premium into account when being able to exercise your options at the right time and make sure the price is high enough above your strike price that you don't end up losing money.

Traders take some time to examine the volatility of a given stock over the recent past, but they also look into what's known as implied volatility. This is a weather forecast for stocks. It's an estimate of the future price movements of a stock, and it has a significant influence on the pricing of options. Implied volatility is denoted by the Greek symbol σ, implied volatility increases in bear markets, and it actually decreases when investors are bullish. Implied volatility is a tool that can provide insight into the options' future value.

While every municipality has its unique tax laws, the following basic principles should be kept in mind as they are generally applicable:

• You are able to sell your primary residence tax-free if you have lived there for two years or more. When investment property is sold, it becomes subject to capital gains tax; additionally, which can reach up to 35%. If you reside in the property for 730 days, not necessarily consecutively, you can also sell it tax-free. If you sell and put the money back into a residence that is equally or more valuable, you won't have to pay taxes on the sale.

Exchanges of investments of the "same kind," or 1031 exchanges, are a useful tool for tax delay. This can be used to swap vacant land for real estate holdings that include a house, a rental property for a business establishment, and so on. The closing needs to happen within 180 days, and you have 45 days to locate up to three different residences. It is advisable to engage a facilitator or an unbiased third party to ensure accurate documentation and handling of funds. • Your primary house cannot be used to accomplish a 1031 exchange. Origination fees and points are permitted, along with loans up to $1 million.

Due to the complexity of tax law, you must seek professional assistance if you find yourself in a unique situation. The money you pay for their services will be multiplied greatly by their industry experience.

One trend in real estate is the movement of buyers into less populated rural areas and away from highly populated metropolitan areas. Aging, well-to-do baby boomers have led to rising property values for vineyards, Bed and breakfasts, horse ranches, and agricultural sites. Rural homes have some disadvantages despite the fact that these locations are good for real estate investment.

It might be challenging to find a home. It may be not easy to locate an investment property at a reasonable price because more people are working from home, and seniors are looking for rural retreats.

It may be challenging to locate trustworthy, knowledgeable, and competitively priced contractors in rural areas. You might have to pay more for qualified employees even though the neighbourhood's average income is lower than the city's.

It isn't easy to place a value on something unique. The worth of many rural residences is essentially guessed because there aren't enough reliable comparisons. Lenders may be reluctant to support a loan for an amazing home since they are aware of this situation. If the buyer can afford a larger down payment and has good credit, this usually won't be an issue. When it comes time to sell a remote investment property, you will have to advertise it throughout a larger area to draw in a pool of prospective buyers who are qualified and interested.

Acknowledging Others Promotes Loyalty Outstanding leaders don't claim their accomplishments. By giving credit when credit is due—and sometimes even when it isn't—they earn people's trust and loyalty. Ronald Reagan is a prime illustration of this. He nearly never took credit for his own achievements, preferring to give his employees the credit instead. By doing this, he won the utmost loyalty from his supporters.

What else is a leader capable of doing? An effective leader can convey a vision to the team that they can all comprehend. That was "Shining City on a Hill" under Reagan. The leader leads the team in achieving the goal. This fosters optimism and increases conviction that the objective can be accomplished.

"Everything is possible for those who believe," as the saying goes. (NIV Mark 9:23

Other Attributes of Outstanding Leaders

Good listeners are frequently great leaders. They don't think they have the greatest or correct solution, so they listen to others instead. They can recognize that a good idea can come from anywhere, at any time, from anyone, and they can also draw from the knowledge and expertise of others. When a great leader finds a concept that makes sense, they listen to the truth within. It could appear as though the concept or thinking "clicks." But timid or insecure people tend to ignore this sense. Great leaders are those who have self-confidence. They possess the confidence to implement superior ideas and are able to recognize when someone has them.

Great leaders have high standards as well. They will not put up with mediocrity. It's hard to play this part since you want people to like you. People might only be a good fit if you push them enough. Reviewing, assessing, and striving for perfection are skills of great leaders. William Welch of General Electric was said to have been an expert at this work and had a reputation for always pushing his staff members to reach the pinnacles of performance. Louis Gerstner, Vince Lombardi, and Winston Churchill all leveraged high expectations to achieve their objectives at IBM. To realize their dreams, they were prepared and able to make the difficult choices.

Regardless of their status as citizens, soldiers, athletes, employees, or players, great leaders treat their people with respect. They are deserving of imitation because they lead by example. They are prepared to go above and beyond to achieve the goals of the institution because they are devoted to it.

Hiring executives who came highly recommended by industry insiders taught me a lot about leadership, according to a man I know who managed a troubled company and then took it to great success. They were a pleasure to collaborate with. They appeared to be competent CEOs who were also articulate and intelligent. But once they were on board, their superiors saw right through them. They saw their new business as a stepping stone to eventually bigger positions. It was a weigh station located on a clearly marked path. Seeing this, the other team members made the decision not to follow their example. They didn't say it out loud, but they knew who was dedicated and who was in charge of the top slot. It took a lot of work. Teams started to doubt the dedication of their leaders.

Earn in a Rising Market

When security prices increase more quickly than the average of the general rate, this is known as a bull market. Bear markets and bull markets both present opportunities for profit-taking, but bear in mind that a bull market does not guarantee success for all investors. Even in a bull market, investing can still result in a loss of money if the right tactics are not used.

A long position in a stock or other security is a common tool in a bull market's toolbox. A long post is the closest thing there is to the proverb "buy low, sell high." It is the simplest investing strategy to describe; all it entails is purchasing a stock at the appropriate moment and selling it when its price approaches its peak. In a bull market, buying low is rather simple; the real difficulty lies in knowing when to sell. While you don't want to sell too soon, you also want to make sure you get all possible earnings. You can utilize an advance/decline ratio to ascertain the future value of any investments you own. You will need to use this strategy in conjunction with attentively examining the sectors in which you have assets because the state of the market as a whole only serves as a partial indicator of your particular holdings. The advance/decline ratio that matters most to you will be unique to technology-based companies if you own predominantly tech stocks. You can choose when to sell your assets by using both strategies, but in general, if the market is doing well overall, but there are fluctuations in your particular sector, now can be a good time to sell or buy a put option with the opportunity to sell later.

Purchasing a stock on call is another well-liked option during a bull market. Consider calls to be the reverse of puts. A call enables you to buy a stock after it has increased in value, whereas a put allows you to sell a stock after it has decreased. In order to reserve the right to sell or purchase a stock under either option, you must pay a premium, but by doing so, you significantly reduce your risk. If you're an investor with more time to watch the markets but need more money to buy a lot of different stocks, you may increase the size of your portfolio by employing a basic call strategy. Buying many call options on equities you think will rise is the method here, and you will redeem one chance when the strike price is reached. If all of the strike prices are born, it is unlikely that you will be able to buy everything because you are spreading your investment across a few different equities. In this instance, you will have forfeited the calls' set price premiums, but you will have gained the ability to wager with a restricted amount of money on several different things. If, after paying the premiums on your other calls, the strike price results in a profit for you, then this has worked to your advantage.

A bull market gives you access to an additional selection of ETFs to invest in, much like a bear market does. The management of these exchange-traded funds is essentially the same: the value of the ETF you own rises proportionately to the performance of a matching index fund. One of the safest ways to earn fair to great interest with no investor involvement is through exchange-traded funds (ETFs) during a bull market. While there are many different exchange-traded funds (ETFs) on the market, the best choice for long-term investors is usually one that aligns with the entire exchange. In terms of pure chance profit, you would have outperformed every investor if you had invested all of your money in a generic Dow Jones Industrial index fund for the final.

The long-term performance of index funds has recently been a point of disagreement for a number of well-known investors. Index funds, according to the argument, are the safest option for investing; yet, other investors and money managers think that investing with a personal touch can yield significantly higher returns. Renowned investor Warren Buffet wagered a million dollars in 2008, claiming that an S&P 500 index fund would gain more than most hedge fund managers could over eight years. The Vanguard 500 index fund increased by 65.67% in the end, whereas the growth of a variety of hedge funds was just 21.87%. The figures were far away. I have only come to believe so strongly in this suggestion. Still, if you have the opportunity to participate in the stock market for ten or more years, the most prudent approach to generate income on your money is through an index fund. When you're ready to take out the Cash, it will give you a sizable nest egg with very little monitoring needed.

Is NFT} A Trend?

A common misconception among consumers is that, considering the nature of digital artwork and avatars, having an NFT is a luxury. For instance, anyone can download a digital artwork that could be sold for millions of dollars and use it for viewing, editing, or other purposes, making NFT trading possible.

Still, you still need to make your painted poster worth $900 million. Similarly, the ownership of an NFT is worth more than a copy, and market forces determine its worth.

The benefits of NFT trading include: ● |
Efficacy   ● | | DĖvisĖbĖlity   ● | |
Transection ● ■ Authentication ● ■
Enhanced artist royalties ● ● ■ ■
Reduced expenses to third parties

The advantages of NFT trading include:
● Environmental considerations ●

Digital wallet requirements ● Young technology.

How to Begin Trading NFTs

Exchange NFT~ First-hand
The easiest and most apparent method to become involved in NFT trading is to purchase and sell NFTs. You must visit a designated marketplace or application in order to locate an NFT for sale. Numerous online marketplaces exist, and the majority of them have slightly different objectives or features.
A digital wallet—though not just any wallet—is also necessary to complete the transaction. Make sure you locate a wallet that supports NFTs, as not all of them can. Once configured, it must be filled with cryptocurrency. At that point, you can use the wallet to purchase any NFT for which you have the necessary funds. After the sale is verified, it will be permanently listed on the blockchain, and the NFT will show up in your wallet.

Putting Money Into The NFT Industry

Trading NFT market tokens or cryptocurrencies is the way to go if you want to get involved in the industry but want to avoid getting directly involved with NFT trading. When a market shrinks, the value of the tokens used to make transactions increases. Certain major markets, like FLOW, can be traded on cryptocurrency exchanges.

In a similar vein, one might trade the cryptocurrency used for NFT trading, such as Ethereum. When ETH is used more frequently for both NFTs and routine purchases, its value increases and profits can be generated by selling tokens.

Decentralization

A slightly more risky method of trading NFTs is through the virtual reality called Decentraland. This is a digital platform that resembles those found in science fiction movies such as Ready Player One. The planet is made up of land parcels, each of which has an NFT that you can purchase to gain ownership.

Parts can be used to create anything you want, from games to advertisements to buildings. The prices of these parts may increase as the planet becomes more populous and more scarce or useful. Parts can be rented out or sold, enabling other creators to place their content there and offering a variety of NFT trading opportunities.

IF AN INVESTMENT DOESN'T WORK

"How much money you make when you're right and how much money you lose when you're wrong matters more than whether you're right or wrong."

(George Soros, philanthropist and billionaire)

It is unrealistic to expect a novice investor to make the proper decisions every time. In actuality, you can't expect to get it perfect all the time! Spreading your risk by investing in a variety of assets is crucial because of this. Even financial experts make mistakes while investing, frequently with disastrous results.

Let's examine seven historical financial scandals to see what lessons can be drawn.

What took place?

Marcus DidiusJulianus was a Roman politician who purchased the Roman Empire from elite soldiers who had vowed to uphold it. He died 66 days later. A little financial commitment!

The Roman Empire, which ruled over portions of Europe and Asia from 753 BC to the 5th century AD, is full of violent legends. A total of 33 emperors were assassinated or put to death.

There were two fallout emperors in 193 AD. Rome's finest troops, known as the Pretorian Guard, killed Emperor Pertinax in order to protect him.

The next emperor died as a result of this assassination, which also sparked a peculiar bidding war within the Empire.

Now that Pertinax had been defeated, these exceptional warriors held the key to the future of the Roman Empire. It was decided to put the empire up for sale to the highest bidder.

Titus Flavius Claudius Sulpicianus, the incumbent Prefect of Rome, promised every soldier 20,000 sesterces in exchange for the reward of the entire Roman Empire. However, Marcus DidiusJulianus, the proconsul of North Africa, outbid him and promised 25,000 sesterces to each Pretorian soldier—nearly six times their yearly salary!

Not surprisingly, the soldiers chose Julianus to be Emperor. The Senate was coerced into giving in.

Julianus's reign of terror was short-lived. He gained enormous unpopularity by purchasing the empire. His sole accomplishment was the depreciation of the Roman money, which ultimately led to hyperinflation and unstable economic conditions. On June 2, 193 AD, a soldier killed Julianus.

Strategies for Investing in Real Estate
We've talked about a lot of different real estate investing themes. Let's now

examine some strategies to bear in mind when investing in real estate.

1. The Rules of Real Estate Investing:

Investing in something exceptional is what you are doing, whether you do it directly or through investment funds. But you can't adhere to the same rules that apply to stock or bond investments. There are specific guidelines for each type of investment, and you must familiarize yourself with them all.

2. Have a plan for leaving:

You ought to be making money whether you are purchasing, selling, or renting out rental properties. But it would be best if you had a plan in place. See whether you can devise a workable plan for your departure. According to Joel Cone, "Real estate investing, like any other investment, necessitates a plan of action."

Sometimes a three-year lease is the goal.
However, your action strategy will be specific to each scenario.

3. Join a neighborhood investment group:

If you collaborate with other investors, you will probably be successful. For this reason, signing up for an investment club is a smart move. On the other hand, avoid wasting your money on unnecessary training programs. All you need to do to learn about real estate investing without having to shell out extra Cash for expensive seminars and camps is to peruse the bookshelves at your neighborhood bookstore.

4. Choose the type of investing that appeals to you:

 It is advised that you choose a certain target market and gather as much information as you can about it. "Set a goal, develop a business plan, and implement mechanisms to attain the intended result," Cone suggested. You should constantly regularly take small measures toward your objectives. But exercise common judgment and talk to the owners, sellers, and even real estate agents in your area.

5. Guard your investments against unforeseen losses:

Put money aside as a safety net in case something unforeseen happens. You will need Cash on hand to fix the ten to fifteen percent of these homes that need repairs every year after you have a substantial portfolio. As you prepare for the best-case situation, consider the worst-case scenario.

Cone stated, "True asset protection comes from insurance." As though the world is destroying them and insurance is their sole line of protection, investors should protect themselves."

6. Direct investment and REIT investment are not the same:

Check the tax ramifications before choosing which to invest in. You must take advantage of tax incentives and capital gains taxes if you want to see a return on your real estate investment. These specifications will change based on the investment you are making.

7. Using funds is a low-maintenance strategy:

A cheap real estate investment option will be offered via mutual funds and exchange-traded funds (ETFs).

8. Your house is not relevant:

Even if your house could seem like an investment, the increase in value will be offset by property taxes and other expenses. Your property does not yield income for you in the same manner as your other investments do.

A real estate investment will either yield income or appreciate in value once all costs are subtracted.

Investing in knowledge and skills

Skills that were formerly necessary for jobs can now be automated. Therefore in order to stay relevant, people need to develop new professional skills.

Even if you might think that your job is unaffected, mechanization has found its way into almost every sector of the economy and every kind of organization. It will be soon that sophisticated machinery and computerization replace about 45% of all jobs worldwide.

This is the time to think about the skills and routines you can develop to ensure that your trip will be safe in the future.

Which Are The Most Important Skills You Should Acquire For The Future?

As you consider the skills you will need Think about what will be useful for your career and what businesses often seek when making acquisitions in the future.

These are the most in-demand skills that you should learn in order to protect your career in the future.

1. Computerized intelligence

It's okay to work in the field of artificial intelligence (AI) to anticipate encountering AI at work.

These advancements are transforming the way businesses operate by raising the bar for representatives with prior experience using computerized reasoning throughout all industries.

Although it doesn't happen overnight, developing artificial intelligence skills is undoubtedly crucial for every firm. The first step towards comprehending the thinking that humans produce is to ascertain its origins. This is essential to understanding how to govern and clarify the reasoning that humans have. You will interact with AI and learn its capabilities after you possess the necessary advancement skills.

2. Programming

Coding has quickly grown to be one of the most sought-after skills that people can learn. Figuring dialects are useful for almost any kind of job and satisfy a variety of purposes. These days, coding is used in so many projects that experts predict it will soon become a necessary core competency.

One skill that can involve considerable investment is learning how to code. How much time it takes you to learn how to code will depend on whatever specific registering language you need to study.

If you must learn to code, begin by looking at several programming languages and evaluating how useful they would be for your line of work.

People usually begin with the easiest dialects to learn, such as HTML or JavaScript. After mastering the foundational dialects, you can move on to more widely used and popular idioms, such as Python.

3. Dispersed processing

Distributed computing provides remote access to organizational stages and is a secure means of storing and managing administrative data.

A few businesses are aware of this breakthrough, which has emerged as the safest method of using and storing information.

If you develop your distributed computing skills, you will have the ability to advise your supervisor on how to manage their cloud. Knowing the different components of the cloud and its prospective applications, from multi-distributed computing to distant information storage, will make you valuable to any firm.

Comprehending the cloud is essential for managing large amounts of data, but on a smaller scale, it is necessary for effectively communicating and supervising specific assignments.

Developing distributed computing skills near crucial tasks, the board talents can help you organize your career and manage organizational procedures.

Errors to Avoid When Investing in Cryptocurrencies

It's always challenging to be new to the world of investing. It's always possible that your inexperience will cause you to make mistakes. You might come to regret the ignorant blunders you committed in the future. We will thus examine the top five errors made by novice investors in the cryptocurrency market.

Dealing with other people

You should be aware of the people you are buying cryptocurrency from if you decide to buy it straight from them rather than through an exchange. Numerous cryptocurrency scams exist when dishonest people claim to have a "stash" of Bitcoin. There have been fake auctions that aim to trick unsuspecting people.

It's usually preferable to have some confirmation that you are speaking with an actual person in situations like this. Indeed, there are instances where cybercriminals pilfer cryptocurrency from other users and then promptly sell it to prospective investors. The true investors are then discovered in possession of the coins and are charged with either carrying out the hack or, at the very least, employing the hackers to do their bidding. It goes without saying that you should steer clear of this at all costs.

Buying unidentified coins

Almost anyone may now create a cryptocurrency. It can be used anywhere and given any name you like. The majority of coins that you locate are used for particular things, like in-game purchases on gaming platforms. That's all very nice. But when you hear about some obscure coin that is being touted as the next great thing (by unknown people), well, then things get dicey.

This is the area where your homework is due.

If the new coin performs well, consider making a small financial investment in it. Only spend a few bucks on a coin that has yet to be verified. You can acquire them for cents on the dollar. Coins only get valued in double digits once they demonstrate that they are desirable to investors and useful in the actual world.

Please be advised that you might need to hang onto the flyer for some time if you decide to take a chance on an unknown coin. If your goal is to make rapid money, you might only achieve a little. In the end, you can find yourself holding a cryptocurrency with little to no future. But since you didn't pay a high amount for it, you would only lose a little on it. For this reason, we consistently emphasize how crucial it is to complete your homework.